Maps
and Mapping

KINGFISHER

Kingfisher Publications Plc
New Penderel House
283–288 High Holborn
London WC1V 7HZ
www.kingfisherpub.com

First published by Kingfisher Publications Plc 2004
4 6 8 10 9 7 5
4TR/0705/PROSP/RNB(RNB)/140MA/F

A CIP catalogue record for this book is
available from the British Library.

ISBN–13: 978 0 7534 0946 6
ISBN–10: 0 7534 0946 1

Senior editor: Belinda Weber
Designer: Peter Clayman
Cover designer: Anthony Cutting
Picture manager: Cee Weston-Baker
Illustrations: Steve Weston, Samuel Weston
Cover illustration: Phoebe Wallman
DTP co-ordinator: Sarah Pfitzner
Artwork archivists: Wendy Allison, Jenny Lord
Senior production controller: Nancy Roberts
Indexer: Chris Bernstein

Printed in China

Acknowledgements
The Publisher would like to thank the following for permission to reproduce their material. Every care has been taken to trace
copyright holders. However, if there have been unintentional omissions or failure to trace copyright holders, we apologise and
will, if informed, endeavour to make corrections in any future edition.
b = bottom, c = centre, l = left, t = top, r = right

Photographs: 2–3 British Library; 4–5 British Library; 8–9 Corbis; 12 Corbis; 14–15t Zefa; 14–15b Corbis; 16 Portuguese Tourist Office;
17 Alamy; 18–19 Getty Images; 19tl Frank Lane Picture Agency; 19br Frank Lane Picture Agency; 20–21 Corbis; 26 Hereford Cathedral;
27 Getty Images; 28 Corbis; 29t Science Photo Library; 29b NASA; 30–31 Science Photo Library; 33t Heritage Image Partnership;
33b Corbis; 34–35 Science Photo Library; 34–35 Science Photo Library; 36 Corbis; 36–37 Science Photo Library; 38–39t Zefa;
38–39b Science Photo Library; 40 Art Archive; 40–41 Science Photo Library; 41 NASA

Commissioned photography on pages 42–47 by Andy Crawford.
Project-maker and photoshoot co-ordinator: Miranda Kennedy.
Thank you to models Lewis Manu and Rebecca Roper.

Maps
and Mapping

Deborah Chancellor

Contents

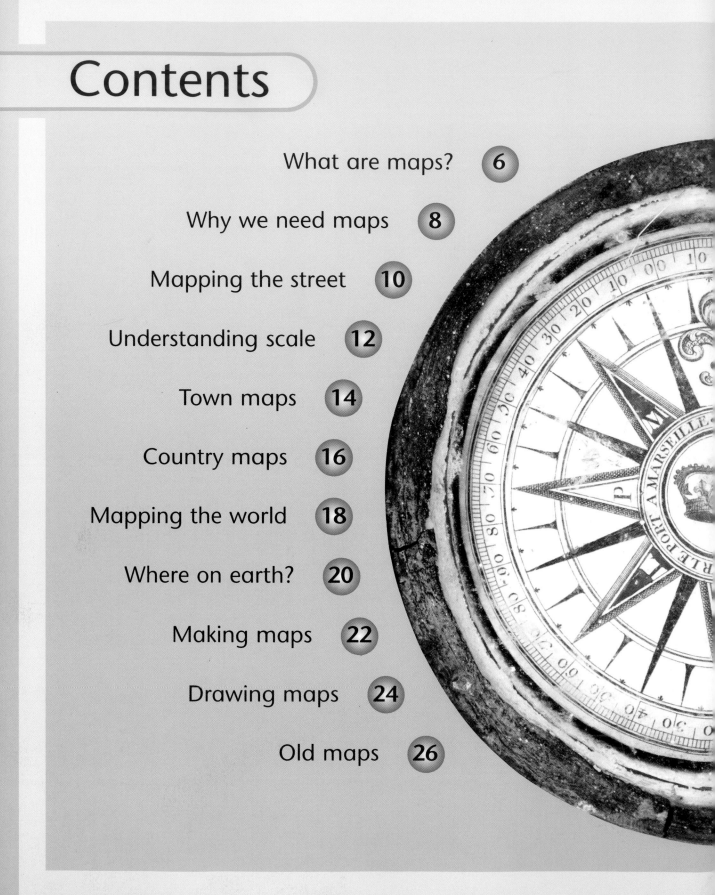

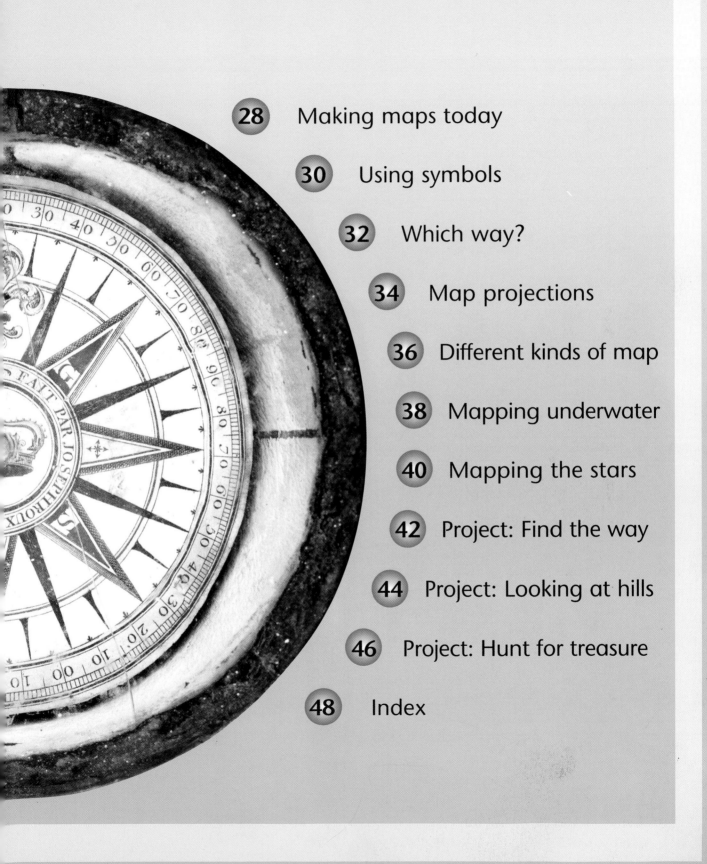

What are maps?

Maps show us what places look like from above. Some maps cover small areas. Others show big countries, or even the whole world.

Learning from maps

Maps give us useful information about countries. This map of Australia shows the main cities, roads and rivers.

Finding places

Maps show us where we are. Grids are put over maps to help us find different places.

How far?

Scale bars on maps show how many kilometres there are per centimetre. You can then measure distances on the map.

grid – pattern of lines that cross each other

1
2
3
4
5
6
7

Perth

4,000m
2,000m
1,000m
500m
200m

A
B
0
800
0
310
620

Darwin

Broome

Cairns

Townsville

Alice Springs

Brisbane

Adelaide

Sydney

Canberra

Melbourne

Hobart

■ Capital city
● City or town
〜 Main road
River

C   D   E   F   G   H   I   J

1600 kilometres

930 miles

Why we need maps

Maps teach us about places. You can spot where countries and continents are on a world map. Important cities are marked with dots, and lines show you where borders are.

continents – enormous masses of land

The world at your fingertips
World maps show the huge
distances between different
countries. When you look at
a world map, you can see how
far away some places are.

__borders__ – boundaries between two countries or states

Mapping the street

We use street maps to find things in a town or city. Street maps look down on a place from above. They show all the buildings, roads and other landmarks.

landmarks – objects that can be seen from a distance

Flat plan

The map above is a plan of the streets in the picture. The buildings and fields are simple, flat shapes. There are no cars or people on the plan.

Understanding scale

Small scale maps show big areas of land and sea. Large scale maps show much smaller areas, in a lot more detail.

Theme park map
This map has a large scale. It gives a lot of detail.

Shrink to fit
Everything on a map has to be shrunk to fit. Small scale maps shrink things even more than large scale maps, so they can show a bigger area.

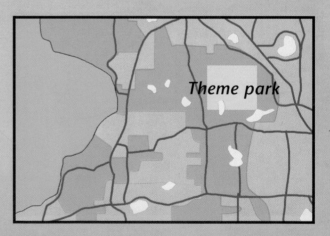

Theme park

Road map
The road map has a smaller scale. It shows where to find the theme park.

area – *part of a place or country*

Orlando •

FLORIDA

UNITED STATES
OF AMERICA

FLORIDA

State map

Our theme park is in
Orlando. This city is just a
dot on a Florida state map.

Country map

This map shows the USA.
It has the smallest scale
on this page.

state – a division of a country

Town maps

We need several different kinds of map in a town or city. If we are walking or driving, street maps are very useful. Bus or train maps help us plan our journeys on public transport.

Finding the way

Tourist maps are sometimes in 3-D. They illustrate the landmarks in a city. The red line on this map shows the route a tourist has planned to find his way around.

Street wise

Buildings and roads look very small on maps, but are much bigger in real life. This busy street in Paris would look very different on a street map.

Train map

On maps of the Metro in Paris, train routes are shown with lines. Each route has its own colour and number. Names of all the stations are marked on the map.

Country maps

Maps of countries cover large areas. They show important features, such as mountains, cities and borders. Symbols on country maps show points of interest.

Capital city

The dots on this map are capital cities. Lisbon is the capital of Portugal. It was built around a natural harbour.

PORTUGAL

● **Lisbon**

capital city – most important city in a country

Natural border

These mountains form a natural border between Spain and France. They are in a mountain range called the Pyrenees.

FRANCE

Borders between countries are marked with a red line

Pyrenees

SPAIN

● **Madrid**

Flamenco dancing

Fishing

Wine making

Orange growing

Water sports

Tourist area

Mapping the world

World maps are covered with a grid of lines. These are lines of latitude and longitude. We use them to work out the exact position of places.

Starting at Greenwich

The 'Greenwich meridian' is the line of longitude that passes through Greenwich, England. It marks 0° (degrees) longitude. All other lines of longitude are measured east or west of this line.

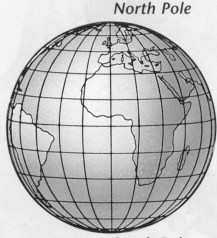

North Pole

South Pole

latitude – *distance north or south of the Equator*

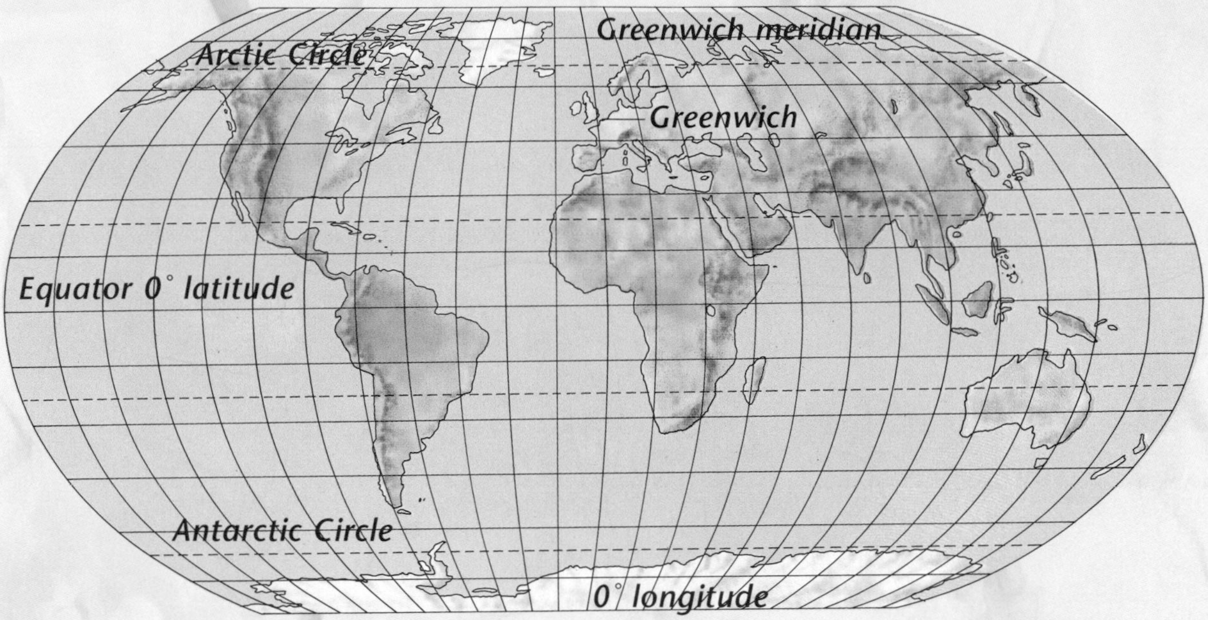

At the poles

All lines of longitude meet at the North and South Poles. These penguins live in the Antarctic, the frozen continent around the South Pole in the Antarctic Circle.

In the middle

The Equator is an imaginary line that runs around the middle of the earth. All lines of latitude are measured north or south of the Equator.

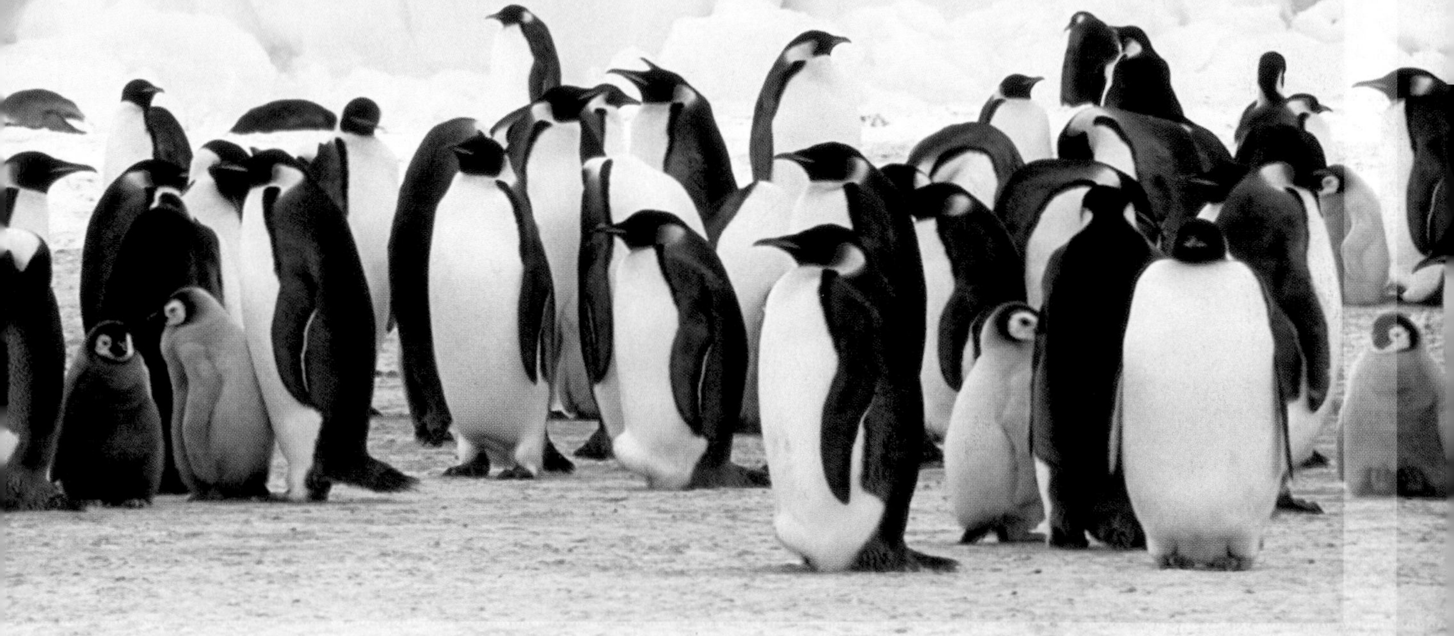

***longitude** – distance east or west of the Greenwich meridian*

Where on earth?

Any position on earth can be described with measurements of latitude and longitude. Grids on maps help us find a particular spot, such as a city on a world map, or buried gold on a treasure map.

Global address

A city's position of latitude and longitude is like an 'address' on a world map. New Orleans in the USA is 30° north and 90° west.

Paddling out to sea

The famous Mississippi river flows through New Orleans and out into the sea. This busy route for river traffic is over 6,000 kilometres long.

position – *exact place where something is*

Finding hiding places

Even treasure maps have grids over them. Any place or thing on the map can be given a 'grid reference', using letters and numbers at the edge of the grid.

A B C D

8

7

6

5

4

3

Forest
River
Beach
Mountain
Volcano
Lake
Swamp
Treasure

X

N
W   E
S

B

C

Making maps

Five hundred years ago, much of the world was unexplored. Brave people discovered unknown lands, and made the first maps of the places they found.

Voyages of discovery

Explorers learned as much as they could about coastlines. They used special equipment to find their way and make maps.

Finding the right way

Compasses helped explorers sail in the right direction. Maps were drawn with north at the top and south at the bottom.

compass

quill pen

Are we there yet?

The distance a ship had
to travel was measured
on a map, using a pair
of dividers.

Where are we now?

Sailors used a sextant
to work out how far
north or south they
were from the Equator.

sextant

dividers

Drawing maps

You need a lot of information about the landscape to draw an exact and correct map. Many measurements must be taken, such as the heights of mountains and the lengths of rivers.

Surveying the land

Surveyors are people who measure features of the landscape, so that maps can be made. They record every detail, for example whether it is woody or bare, dry or marshy.

Contour lines

On some maps, hills and mountains are shown with 'contour lines'. These lines link all the land that is the same height. The closer the lines, the steeper the slope.

landscape – *area of the countryside*

Old maps

People have been making maps for thousands of years. The first maps of the whole world were made about 1,800 years ago. They only show countries and oceans that were known about at the time.

What's missing?

The first map-makers did not know that America, Australia and the Antarctic existed. This map shows what some people thought the world looked like about 900 years ago.

Changing maps

World maps changed when new countries were found. This map was made about 100 years after America was first 'discovered'.

Modern map

This is a modern map of the world. There are no new lands left to explore, and we know what all the continents look like. Today, nothing is missing from our maps.

ocean – a large sea

Making maps today

New technology helps us make maps. Photographs of land and sea can be taken from aircraft and satellites. Cartographers use these images and other information to create maps.

Using computers

Today, cartographers use computers to help them make maps. Lots of geographical data can be stored on a database and used to create many different kinds of map. This is a digital map of part of Asia.

Eyes in the sky

This is a Russian space satellite, circling high above the earth. Data from many satellites is sent back to earth and is used to make maps.

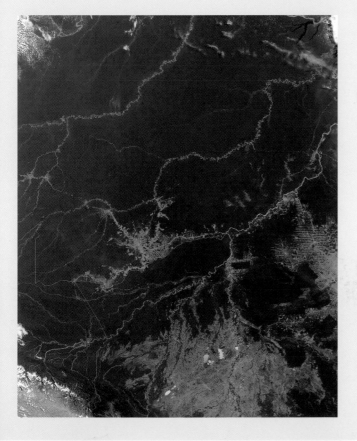

Looking down

The Amazon river in northern Brazil looks like this from space. The dark areas are rainforest, and the river is a thin yellow line. Satellite photos give cartographers a detailed picture of the landscape.

cartographers – people who draw maps

Using symbols

Maps have to crowd a lot of information into a small space. Symbols and colours on maps are used to show many different things on the ground.

Flying over London

This is bird's eye view of central London. Street maps of the area show all the roads, buildings and parks. Symbols tell us what important buildings are used for.

Map key

Symbols and colours on maps are explained in a key. We need to look at the key to understand what the map is showing us.

P	Car park
i	Information
⊖	Underground
▭	Police station
+	Hospital
	Park
	Housing area
	Business area
✡	Synagogue
☾	Mosque
+	Church

bird's eye view – *picture of something from above*

Up close

This map shows a small area of the satellite photo. Different colours show how land is used, for example for houses or parks.

key – *explanation of symbols on a map*

Which way?

Whichever way you look, you are facing in a particular direction. This will be somewhere between north, south, east and west. You use a compass to find your direction.

Map reading

These hikers are using a compass with a map. They turn the map around, so the north arrow lines up with the compass needle.

Pointing the way

All maps have an arrow
or 'compass rose' on them,
showing north. In Lisbon,
and other places, the
compass directions are
shown on the ground, too.

Go north

You need to use a compass
to discover which way
is north. A compass has
a magnetic needle that
always points towards
the north.

Map projections

The most accurate world maps are globes, because they show the land and sea as it really is. Flat maps change the shape of some countries.

Projections

The way we show the curved earth on a flat map is called a projection. The projection on the right is the 'Mercator' projection.

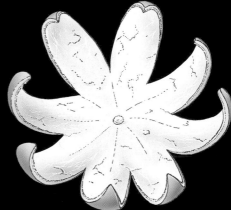

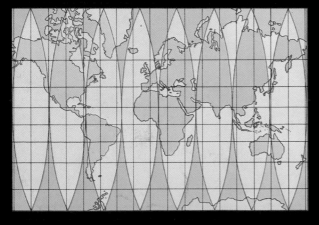

Flat map

A globe can be split into segments and 'peeled' like an orange. The segments are placed side by side to make a flat map that looks like this.

globe – ball with a map of the world on it

Different views

There are many different map projections. The one below cuts the globe up in a special way, so countries and oceans are not too distorted.

distorted – *changed from normal shape*

Different kinds of map

There are many kinds of map. Maps can give information about things, such as the weather. They can also show how places compare with each other.

Underwater maps

Maps of the sea are called charts. They help boats follow routes and avoid dangers. The crosses on this chart stand for shipwrecks on the seabed.

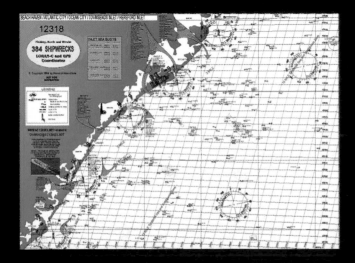

chart – map of the sea, sky or space

Mapping the weather

Weather maps tell us what the weather is like in a particular place. Symbols are used to show different types of weather. The symbols here show sun, clouds, rain and tornadoes.

Night lights

This world map was made using many satellite photos. It shows which parts of the world use the most electric light at night.

routes – *ways to go to get to a place*

Mapping underwater

There are huge mountains and deep canyons under the sea. Measurements of these features are taken, so that maps showing the ocean floor can be made.

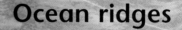

Ocean ridges

Underwater mountain ranges are called ocean ridges. They can be very long. On this map, the deepest water is dark blue. The ocean ridges are the lightest blue.

ridges – ranges of mountains

Deep blue sea

Special equipment measures how long sound takes to reach the seabed and bounce back again. Then, the depth of the water can be worked out.

Diving for data

Deep sea submersibles are small submarines that take divers down to explore the seabed. Measurements are taken by divers to provide data for maps.

submersibles – craft that can travel underwater

Mapping the stars

People who study stars in the sky are called astronomers. Today, astronomers look at distant galaxies through powerful telescopes. Then they make space maps, called star charts.

Seeing stars

You can look at the stars with a simple pair of binoculars. Some constellations are seen from the northern half of the world, and others from the south.

galaxies – *very large groups of stars*

Star charts

Long ago, people named constellations after animals, heroes and gods. They painted beautiful charts to show the position of the stars in the sky.

Mapping the moon

Maps are made of the moon as well as the earth. Photographs are used to make maps of the craters, valleys and canyons on the surface of the moon.

constellations – *groups of stars*

Find the way

Make your own compass

A compass needle is a magnet that points north. You can turn a needle into a magnet, and float it in water to make a compass.

You will need
- Large needle
- Magnet
- Cork
- Tub of water
- Compass

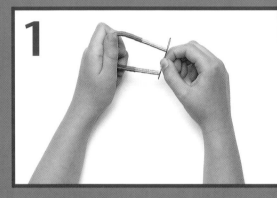

1

Hold the needle and gently stroke it with the magnet. Do this about 50 times, always stroking in the same direction.

2

Ask an adult to cut a slice of cork for you. Carefully balance your pin on the cork and float it in a tub of water.

3

Place a compass next to your floating needle. Both 'compass needles' should be facing in the same direction – north!

Mapping your bedroom

You can draw a map of your bedroom, using your footsteps to measure what is there. Count how many footsteps it takes to walk the length and width of your room. You will need some paper, a ruler and some felt-tip pens to make your map.

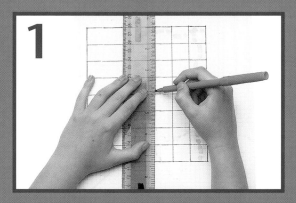

1

Draw an outline of your room. Fill it in with a grid. Each square on the grid stands for one footstep.

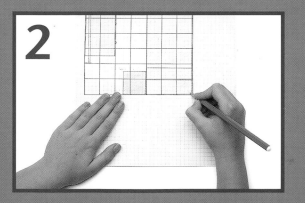

2

Measure your furniture in footsteps. Draw furniture shapes on your map, putting them in the right places.

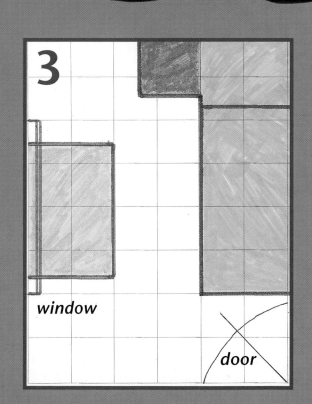

3

window

door

Add the door and window. Colour all the furniture using felt-tip pens. You can draw a map key to explain your colours.

Looking at hills

Make a relief map

Some maps use colour shading and modelling
to show how land varies in height. Mountains
and valleys are easy to see on a relief map.
You can make a relief map with craft materials.

Roll up three balls of newspaper.
Make each ball a different size.
Stick the balls firmly to the thick
cardboard, using sticky tape.

You will need
- Newspaper
- Sheet of thick card
- Sticky tape
- Scissors
- Glue or wallpaper paste
- Kitchen paper
- Poster paints
- Paintbrush

Cut some pieces of newspaper into
thin strips. Glue the strips over the
newspaper balls. Add several
layers, then leave them to dry.

3

Glue a layer of kitchen paper over the map. Remember to cover the cardboard base as well as the 'hills'. Leave to dry.

4

Paint your map with bands of colour. Use a new colour to show different heights. Land of the same height should be the same colour.

On this map, green shows low ground. Yellow shades stand for medium height while dark brown means higher ground.

Hunt for treasure

Make a treasure map

In stories, old maps of desert islands help people find buried treasure. Make your own treasure map for a fantasy island.

Scrunch a piece of paper into a loose ball. Flatten it out again with your hands.

You will need
- Paper
- Poster paints
- Paintbrush
- Pencil
- Ruler
- Felt-tip pens
- Scissors

Dilute some green or brown paint to make it very watery. Paint a wash over the whole sheet of crumpled paper. Leave to dry.

Draw a grid of squares over the paper with a pencil and ruler. Each line should be the same distance apart.

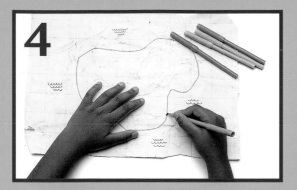

4

Draw the outline of a desert island. Make it an interesting, unusual shape. Add some waves to show where the sea is.

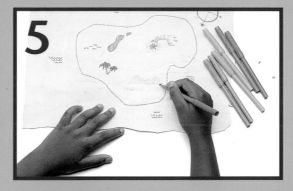

5

Draw some pictures on your map to stand for different things, such as lakes and volcanoes. Make the symbols small and simple.

6

Draw a key to explain your symbols, and add a north arrow. Shade the edges to make the map look old.

Ask your friends to work out where the treasure is buried.

Index